Oh Little Stone

written by
Joshua Anderson Taylor

illustrated by
Anna Perevalova
&
Joshua Anderson Taylor

First hardback edition August 2022

Original artwork by Anna Perevalova
Adjusted by Joshua Anderson Taylor

ISBN 978-1-3999-2649-2 (hardback)

www.joshuaandersontaylor.com

for
Emilie
and
Hendy

May we never be
ducks in the night.

As I walked along the beach one day,
I saw a stone, all alone,
on the sand by the bay.

He was plain and round,
and reddish brown,
not a special stone was he.

Just a stone,

all alone,

sitting quietly by the sea.

'A **puzzle**!' said I, as I wondered why
this stone was by the sea.
For gone was the tide
and the beach was very wide
and no other had I seen
for a mile on either side...

...so a very special stone indeed,
thought I, was he.

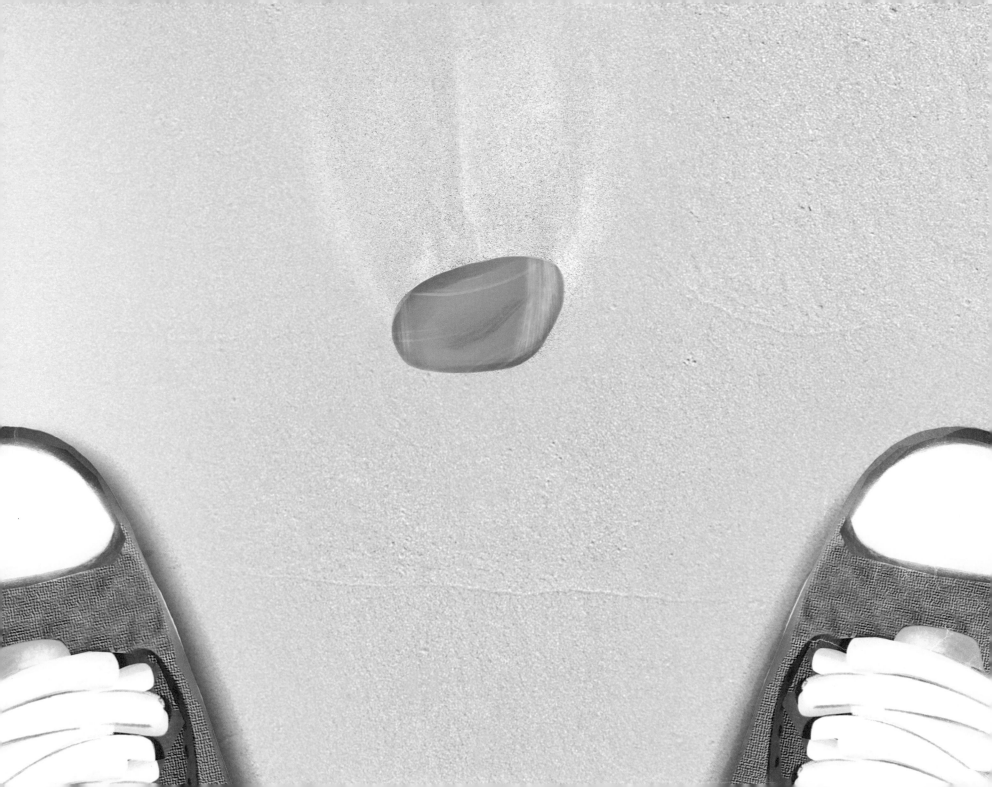

I then did something I've never done before,
and I've never done it since,
though I wish I did it more.

It may have looked quite silly,

and a little bit amiss,

but I started talking to the stone

and what I said was this...

"Oh little stone,
what is your story?

Have you seen great things,
of wonder and glory?

What have you seen?

What have you heard?

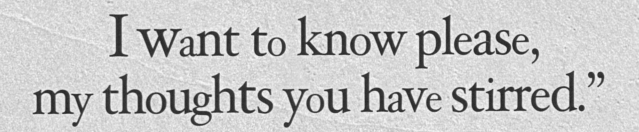

I want to know please,
my thoughts you have stirred."

Were you there, little stone,
when the world was brand new,

and hot lava rocks
flamed, fizzled
and flew?

Were you there, little stone,
for the first drops of rain...

...and when the rivers rushed
down from the peaks to the plain?

Were you there, little stone,
for the first of the
floWers,

for the plants **BIG** as shields
...and the trees tall as towers?

Did you ever hear, little stone, a dinosaur **R O A R**
or see it **stomp** or *snap* or ha**tch** or *CLAW?*

Were you there, little stone, when the mammals took charge?

The small and the scrappy, the hairy, the large!

Were you ever, little stone, the tip of a spear
when those Strange things called humans appeared?

What was it like when they made the first flames, spoke the first words and played the first games?

Were you there, little stone,
for the wars beyond **count**?

Did you **cower**
at the **CLASH**

and the *BANG*

and the *SHOUT?*

Have you seen, little stone,
all our marvellous inventions

like bicycles and basketballs,
and cars with suspensions?

Do you like, little stone,
how **clever** we've got?

Do you think us
wise and **wonderful**
or do you think **not**?

It was then that I stopped talking,
for I was late for tea.
So I left my stone and started home,
my mind as stirred as stirred can be.

But no sooner had I walked
but ten yards or twelve or more
when I turned in curiousity
and gasped at what I saw...

...for the stone I had been talking to
was on the sand

no more.

There was nothing.
Just the sand and me.

All alone,

without a stone,

standing quietly
by the Sea.

For years
I kept on
walking...

...across beach and hill and glen,

but never did I see
that little stone again.

But every now and then
when my mind can wander free,
I remember my stone, all alone,
sitting quietly by the sea
and smile...

...for a very special stone was he.

joshuaandersontaylor.com

Lightning Source UK Ltd.
Milton Keynes UK
UKRC031242051022
409967UK00001B/11